Congressional
Research
Service

Securing Nuclear Materials: The 2012 Summit and Issues for Congress

Mary Beth Nikitin
Specialist in Nonproliferation

March 7, 2012

Congressional Research Service

7-5700

www.crs.gov

R41169

Summary

In an April 2009 speech in Prague, President Obama pledged that his Administration would launch "a new international effort to secure all vulnerable nuclear material around the world within four years." To motivate world leaders to achieve this goal, the President hosted a Nuclear Security Summit in Washington, DC, on April 12-13, 2010. Leaders of 47 countries attended the summit, including many heads of state. Attendees represented a wide geographic range of states and nuclear capabilities, and include China, India, Israel, and Pakistan. The summit resulted in a joint statement saying that international cooperative action is necessary to prevent an act of nuclear terrorism. Summit attendees also pledged to improve nuclear security standards, bring international agreements into force, and share best practices. A second summit will be held in South Korea in March 2012.

Nuclear security measures refer to a wide range of actions to prevent theft or diversion of nuclear material or sabotage at an installation or in transit. They could include physical protection measures, material control and accounting, personnel reliability screening, and training. A broader understanding of nuclear security also includes measures to prevent and detect illicit trafficking— cargo inspections, border security, and interdiction measures.

The U.S. government has worked for more than a decade both domestically and in partnership with other countries to address this problem through multiple programs at the Departments of Defense, Energy, Homeland Security, and State. The International Atomic Energy Agency has also played a lead role in these efforts, particularly since the 9/11 terrorist attacks.

Congress will continue to decide on funding for the U.S. domestic and international programs focused on nuclear material security and nuclear terrorism prevention. Congress is also likely to assess implementation of the Administration's efforts to secure nuclear materials by the end of 2013. The Obama Administration's FY2011, FY2012, and FY2013 congressional budget requests proposed overall increases in funding for nuclear security-related accounts, with the stated purpose of ramping up programs to meet the President's four-year goal.

Contents

Tables

Appendixes

Contacts

Introduction

In an April 2009 speech in Prague, President Obama said that nuclear terrorism is the "most immediate and extreme threat to global security," and announced "a new international effort to secure all vulnerable nuclear material around the world within four years."[1] To mobilize world leaders to meet this goal, the President hosted a Nuclear Security Summit in Washington, DC, on April 12-13, 2010. Heads of state from 47 countries gathered to lay out their priorities and focus the world's attention on the issue.

The Obama Administration's April 2010 Nuclear Posture Review Report confirms nuclear terrorism as topping the list of nuclear dangers to the United States: "The vulnerability to theft or seizure of vast stocks of such nuclear materials around the world, and the availability of sensitive equipment and technologies in the nuclear black market, create a serious risk that terrorists may acquire what they need to build a nuclear weapon."[2]

Securing nuclear materials is seen by many as crucial to preventing an act of nuclear terrorism.[3] The nuclear terrorism threat can be divided into four categories: an attack using a stolen nuclear weapon, an attack using fissile material in an improvised nuclear device (IND), an attack using a radiological dispersal devise (RDD), and sabotage against a nuclear power plant.[4] Nuclear security practices would be necessary to prevent each of these scenarios.

The IND scenario would require that a terrorist group obtain weapons-usable fissile material (highly enriched uranium or plutonium). Because production of fissile material is costly and equipment relatively difficult to obtain, many believe that terrorist groups would not be able to produce weapon-usable nuclear material and would therefore need to steal or purchase the material or weapon from a state. Therefore, the United States has made it a policy priority to secure nuclear material where it is housed or remove the material from sites around the world.

Nuclear security measures refer to a wide range of actions to prevent theft or diversion of nuclear material or sabotage at an installation or in transit. They could include physical protection measures, material control and accounting, personnel reliability screening, and training. A broader understanding of nuclear security also includes measures to prevent and detect illicit trafficking—cargo inspections, border security, and interdiction measures. Another aspect, "nuclear security culture," describes personnel attitudes towards the importance of nuclear security practices in their daily work.

The United States government has worked both domestically and in partnership with other countries to address this problem through multiple programs at the Departments of Defense, Energy, Homeland Security, and State. The International Atomic Energy Agency has also played a lead role in these efforts, particularly since the 9/11 terrorist attacks. Congressional interest in this

---

[1] Remarks by President Obama, Prague, April 5, 2009. Full text at http://www.whitehouse.gov/the_press_office/Remarks-By-President-Barack-Obama-In-Prague-As-Delivered/.

[2] http://www.defense.gov/npr/docs/2010%20Nuclear%20Posture%20Review%20Report.pdf.

[3] This report does not assess the likelihood of a terrorist nuclear attack. For an overview, see CRS Report RL32595, *Nuclear Terrorism: A Brief Review of Threats and Responses*, by Jonathan Medalia.

[4] Ferguson, Potter, et al., *The Four Faces of Nuclear Terrorism*. October 2005, http://cns.miis.edu/books/4faces.htm.

issue is centered around preventing a nuclear terrorist attack against the United States and providing funding for related programs.

The 2012 Seoul Summit

The South Korean government has said that its main objectives for the 2012 Nuclear Security Summit are to enhance cooperative measures to combat nuclear terrorism, to encourage protection of nuclear materials and related facilities, and to prevent illicit trafficking.[5] The 2012 summit attendees may also broaden the scope of the discussion to include radiological material security, information security, and the interrelationship of nuclear security and nuclear safety in the wake of the Fukushima nuclear accident in Japan last year. The role of the International Atomic Energy Agency in facilitating states' implementation of nuclear security measures will also be emphasized. The Netherlands has agreed to host a third Nuclear Security Summit in 2014, creating another opportunity to measure progress. As with the 2010 summit, participants are expected to make announcements about how their country will contribute to nuclear security in the intervening years.

The 2010 Washington Summit

President Obama has said that at the April 2010 Nuclear Security Summit, "we will advance our goal of securing all of the world's vulnerable nuclear materials within four years."[6] Secretary of State Hillary Clinton has called the summit "an unprecedented gathering that will help promote a common understanding of the threat of nuclear terrorism and build international support for effective means of countering that threat."[7]

Leaders of 47 countries attended the summit, including many heads of state.[8] The attendees represented a wide geographic range of states. Their experience with nuclear security issues ranges from countries that possess nuclear weapons, those that have nuclear energy programs, and others that are potential transshipment points for illicit trafficking. Representatives from the IAEA, the United Nations, and the European Union also attended.

The summit resulted in a joint statement with a pledge to improve nuclear security standards and share best practices, and confirmed agreement that international action is necessary to prevent an act of nuclear terrorism. Vice President Biden described the timing of the meeting as thus: "We

---

[5] The official website of the Seoul summit can be found at http://www.thenuclearsecuritysummit.org/eng_main/main.jsp.

[6] President Barack Obama Delivers Remarks at Suntory Hall, Tokyo, Japan, *CQ Transcripts*, November 14, 2009.

[7] Secretary of State Hillary Clinton Remarks at the United States Institute of Peace, October 21, 2009, http://www.state.gov/secretary/rm/2009a/10/130806 htm.

[8] Attendees included Algeria, Argentina, Armenia, Australia, Belgium, Brazil, Canada, Chile, China, the Czech Republic, Egypt, Finland, France, Georgia, Germany, India, Indonesia, Israel, Italy, Japan, Jordan, Kazakhstan, Malaysia, Mexico, Morocco, Netherlands, New Zealand, Nigeria, Norway, Pakistan, Philippines, Poland, the Republic of Korea, the Russian Federation, Saudi Arabia, Singapore, Switzerland, South Africa, Spain, Sweden, Thailand, Turkey, United Arab Emirates, the United Kingdom, Ukraine, and Vietnam. White House Press Briefing, April 6, 2010.

---

cannot wait for an act of nuclear terrorism before coming together to share best practices and raise security standards, and we will seek firm commitments from our partners to do just that."[9]

The summit concentrated on the goal of securing weapons-usable nuclear materials (highly enriched uranium and plutonium), and did not address nuclear weapons security issues specifically. Focusing on nuclear materials may have been in part to secure the participation of states most sensitive to discussing nuclear weapons issues. Radiological material security was also not emphasized, although many nuclear security practices relevant to weapons-usable nuclear materials are also relevant to other nuclear materials, including radiological sources in the civilian fuel cycle.

Summit Outcomes

Summit participants discussed the nuclear terrorism threat and "steps that can be taken together to secure vulnerable materials, combat nuclear smuggling and deter, detect, and disrupt attempts at nuclear terrorism."[10] The summit also highlighted the role of the IAEA and the nuclear industry in promoting nuclear security best practices.

According to White House summaries, the outcome of the summit was to be a communiqué "pledging efforts to attain the highest levels of nuclear security, which is essential for international security as well as the development and expansion of peaceful nuclear energy worldwide."[11] Summit documents endorse the key international treaties and multilateral initiatives dealing with nuclear security (detailed below). President Obama, in an April 5, 2010, interview said he expected "a communiqué that spells out very clearly, here's how we're going to achieve locking down all the nuclear materials over the next four years, and different countries, depending on their circumstances and vulnerabilities, taking very specific steps in order to assure that that happens."[12] The summit documents included a work plan with specific follow-up steps.[13]

Additional benefits resulted from the meeting apart from summit policy documents. In the run-up to the summit, participating governments examined their own nuclear security and export control practices, their use of weapons-usable materials in the civilian fuel cycle, and in some cases, their ability to provide nuclear security assistance to other countries. This preparatory process could have spurred some countries to make progress to present at the summit[14]—for example, just prior to the summit, Chile, with U.S. assistance, removed the remaining HEU at research facilities;[15]

---

[9] "The Path to Nuclear Security: Implementing the President's Prague Agenda," Remarks of Vice President Joseph Biden at the National Defense University, February 18, 2010, http://www.whitehouse.gov/the-press-office/remarks-vice-president-biden-national-defense-university.

[10] "Addressing the Nuclear Threat: Fulfilling the Promise of Prague at the L'Aquila Summit," White House Press Release, July 8, 2009, http://www.whitehouse.gov/the_press_office/Addressing-the-Nuclear-Threat-Fulfilling-the-Promise-of-Prague-at-the-LAquila-Summit/.

[11] Ibid., White House Press Release, July 8, 2009. The full text of the communiqué can be found at http://www.whitehouse.gov/the-press-office/communiqu-washington-nuclear-security-summit.

[12] "Excerpts from Obama Interview," *The New York Times*, April 5, 2010.

[13] Work Plan of the Washington Nuclear Security Summit, http://www.whitehouse.gov/the-press-office/work-plan-washington-nuclear-security-summit.

[14] A full list can be found at "Highlights of the National Commitments Made at the Nuclear Security Summit," White House Press Release, April 13, 2010, http://www.whitehouse.gov/the-press-office/highlights-national-commitments-made-nss.

[15] "Ahead of Nuclear Summit, NNSA Announces Removal of All Highly Enriched Uranium from Chile," NNSA Press (continued...)

Malaysia passed national export control legislation;[16] Ukraine announced on April 12 that it would remove all HEU from its territory and convert its research reactor to LEU fuel, with U.S. assistance, by 2012;[17] and Canada's prime minister announced the return of HEU spent fuel to the United States.[18] Canada and the United States announced a trilateral agreement with Mexico to convert its HEU-fueled research reactor to LEU fuel.[19] The United States and Russia reached agreement on plutonium disposition,[20] and Russia announced a shut-down of its last remaining plutonium production reactor. Kazakhstan completed work with the United States on moving sensitive material to more secure storage in November 2010. Many of these initiatives had been long-term objectives of the United States, and the summit seems to have moved stalled negotiations forward. Obama Administration officials said that almost every country came to the summit with something new that they pledged to accomplish on nuclear security in their country.

The composition of the meeting was also important. Three states not party to the Non-Proliferation Treaty (NPT) were in attendance—Pakistan, Israel,[21] and India. Holding discussions of nuclear security outside the NPT context allows these countries to participate. Egypt's participation was also a key endorsement of the nuclear security agenda due to its vocal role in the Non-Aligned Movement, where skepticism of the nuclear terrorism threat runs highest. In addition, the Russian Federation said it would be helping the United States prepare the groundwork for the conference. The United States and Russia have a history of cooperating on nuclear material security and nuclear terrorism prevention, announcing the Global Initiative to Combat Nuclear Terrorism together, and fulfilling bilateral nuclear security pledges under the Bratislava Initiatives. Since Russia holds the world's largest stockpiles of weapons-usable nuclear material, it may be beneficial to continue this partnership at a high political level to ensure follow-through with past pledges and further progress in the future.

In addition to nuclear material security goals, the summit has the potential to strengthen the overall nonproliferation regime. China, for example, has in the past been cautious in discussing these issues but announced the creation of a nuclear security "Center of Excellence" to share best practices with developing countries. Participation of the non-NPT states in discussions about the nuclear terrorism threat may lay the groundwork for future discussions on nonproliferation and export control initiatives. Some analysts in India, for example, are changing the conventional

---

(...continued)

Release, April 8, 2010, http://nnsa.energy.gov/news/2894 htm.

[16] "Malaysia Finally Adopts Export Controls," ISIS Report, April 9, 2010, http://isis-online.org/isis-reports/detail/malaysia-finally-adopts-national-export-controls/.

[17] Fact Sheet on Ukraine's Non-proliferation Efforts, the White House website, April 12, 2010, http://www.whitehouse.gov/sites/default/files/Fact%20Sheet%20on%20Ukraine%20HEU%20announcement_FINAL%20(4-12-10).pdf.

[18] "PM announces a nuclear cooperation project with the United States to further secure inventories of spent highly enriched uranium," press release, Office of the Prime Minister of Canada, April 12, 2010, http://www.pm.gc.ca/eng/media.asp?category=1&id=3278.

[19] "Mexico to convert reactor to low-enriched uranium," *Associated Press*, April 13, 2010.

[20] http://www.whitehouse.gov/the-press-office/highlights-national-commitments-made-nss.

[21] The Israeli government announced on April 8, 2010, that Deputy Prime Minister Dan Meridor planned to attend the summit instead of Prime Minister Netanyahu. Press reports quote an Israeli official as saying that the Prime Minister decided not to attend due to concerns that Egypt or Turkey would use the forum to call on Israel to accede to the Non-Proliferation Treaty. However, some analysts believe that Netanyahu may not be ready to respond to recent White House requests for actions related to jump-starting the Israeli-Palestinian peace process. "Netanyahu to Skip Obama Summit," Politico, April 8, 2010, http://www.politico.com/news/stories/0410/35561 html.

---

thinking about some aspects of nonproliferation (i.e., as a common good rather than a way to suppress their weapons ambitions). India announced it would create a regional nuclear energy training center with a nuclear security component.[22] At the highest political level, through the summit process, countries are questioning how their country can help prevent a nuclear terrorism attack from occurring.

However, although all countries may agree that nuclear terrorism should be prevented, many developing countries, particularly those without nuclear programs, do not view nuclear terrorism as a threat to their country, see its occurrence as unlikely, or simply are occupied with other priorities. However, others argue that it is important to gain the participation of all states, as any country could potentially be used as a transshipment point or may choose to develop nuclear-related facilities on its territory one day. Administration officials said that preparations for the summit and the meeting itself have bridged gaps in threat perceptions.[23] The summit participants continue to meet to prepare for the next nuclear security summit in 2012, hosted by South Korea.

Select Accomplishments Since the 2010 Nuclear Security Summit

- **Global Cleanout.** According to NSC official Laura Holgate, "Since this lockdown strategy was announced, about 20 sites around the world containing thousands of kilograms of nuclear materials—enough for several hundred nuclear weapons—have been cleaned out."[24] DOE press releases cite that six countries have removed all of the HEU in their countries since President Obama's 2009 Prague speech. This includes the following:

  - Serbia: On December 22, 2010, DOE announced the removal of 13 kg of Russian-origin HEU spent fuel from the Vinca Institute of Nuclear Sciences. This completes a nine-year cleanout process.

  - Ukraine: On December 31, 2010, DOE announced the removal of 50 kg of HEU fresh fuel from three sites in Ukraine. In May 2010, 56 kg of Russian-origin HEU spent fuel was removed to Russia. These steps partly fulfill Ukraine's commitment at the Nuclear Security Summit to remove all of Ukraine's HEU by 2012.

  - Belarus: In December 2010, the government of Belarus, in a joint statement with the United States, announced that it would eliminate all its HEU stocks by the 2012 Nuclear Security Summit. The *Washington Post* reported that the United States had already worked with Belarus to remove HEU at the Sosny research reactor prior to the December announcement, in classified operations.

  - Mexico: The United States is working with Canada on plans to convert an HEU-fueled research reactor in Mexico.

  - Vietnam: In December 2010, the United States and Vietnam established a legal framework for U.S.-Vietnam cooperation for full conversion of the Dalat research reactor and the return of HEU spent fuel to Russia.

  - Kazakhstan: In November 2010, the United States and Kazakhstan completed the final shipment of HEU and Pu to a secured storage site from the aging BN-350 reactor. This ends a cleanout effort that began over a decade ago. The spent fuel contained 10 metric tons of HEU and 3 metric tons of weapons-grade plutonium.[25]

  - Czech Republic: In June 2010, HEU fresh fuel was removed from the REZ facility.

  - South Africa: On August 16, 2011, DOE announced the removal of 6.3 kg of U.S.-origin HEU spent fuel from a research facility in South Africa. Technical work continues on converting Mo-99 production to LEU

---

[22] "India N-Centre to Have 4 Schools," *The Asian Age*, April 14, 2010.

[23] Press Briefing by Rhodes, Samore, Holgate, Washington Convention Center, April 13, 2010.

[24] Laura Holgate, "Meeting President Obama's Goal of Securing All Loose Nuclear Material around the World by 2012," Comments at the Third Annual Nuclear Deterrence Summit, February 17, 2011.

[25] NNSA Press Release, November 18, 2010, http://nnsa.energy.gov/mediaroom/speeches/harringtonbn350.

fuel, as pledged at the Summit.

- **Work continues in Russia** "to complete comprehensive upgrades at about 40 buildings and sites and continuing improvements in transportation security and guard force support." In fall 2010, Russia and the United States developed a plan to sustain upgraded physical protection systems at MOD sites. Russia has also eliminated almost 2 tons of HEU removed from other countries. Russia also announced it would conduct a study on the feasibility of converting its HEU-fueled research reactors to LEU. The United States and Russia signed a Plutonium Management and Disposition (PMDA) protocol in April 2010, and it entered into force in July 2011.

- **Training centers**, called "Centers for Excellence," focused on nuclear security announced in Japan, China, India, and South Korea.

- **Nuclear smuggling** and border security training held in numerous countries.

- **IAEA** published a new revision of its guidelines for physical protection (INFCIRC/225/Revision 5). Additional Nuclear Security Series booklets were also published for member states.

- **U.S. domestic** removal recently included cleaning excess nuclear materials from Sandia National Laboratory. The United States invited the IAEA to conduct an IPPAS mission at the National Institute of Standards and Technology (NIST) Center for Neutron Research, which will convert its HEU research reactor to LEU fuel.

What Is "Nuclear Security"?

The 2010 Nuclear Security Summit focused on efforts to secure nuclear weapons-usable materials (highly enriched uranium and plutonium) and broader efforts to prevent nuclear terrorism. However, the phrase "nuclear security" is often associated with the security of nuclear weapons.[26] "Nuclear security" has also been used to describe the role of nuclear weapons in national security, including maintaining the U.S. nuclear weapons arsenal. For example, Vice President Biden's March 2010 speech at National Defense University, "Pathways to Nuclear Security," addressed both stockpile stewardship and nuclear nonproliferation efforts. The NNSA refers to a modernized U.S. nuclear weapons complex as the "21st Century Nuclear Security Enterprise." NNSA Administrator Thomas D'Agostino testified that the enterprise's future "range of missions include stockpile stewardship, nonproliferation and disarmament, arms control and treaty verification, counterterrorism and emergency response, nuclear forensics, and Naval nuclear propulsion."[27] Still others use the term "nuclear security" to characterize a vision of a safer world without nuclear weapons.[28]

Nuclear security for the purpose of the summit, and in the International Atomic Energy Agency's usage, refers to a wide range of measures to prevent theft or diversion of nuclear material or sabotage at civilian or military facilities. The measures could protect material at an installation or in transit, such as physical protection measures, material control and accounting, personnel reliability screening, and training. A broader understanding of nuclear security also includes

---

[26] Criticism by other countries (and domestically) of the U.S. nuclear security record often cites security lapses in custody of nuclear weapons themselves such as the 2007 Minot incident. See "Safety, Security and Management Issues" in CRS Report RL33640, *U.S. Strategic Nuclear Forces: Background, Developments, and Issues,* by Amy F. Woolf.

[27] Thomas D'Agostino, Testimony before the House Appropriations Committee, Subcommittee on Energy and Water, March 4, 2010, http://nnsa.energy.gov/news/2855.htm.

[28] http://www.nuclearsecurityproject.org/site/c.mjJXJbMMIoE/b.3534665/k.5828/About_the_Project_Index.htm.

measures to detect illicit trafficking—cargo inspections, customs, and border security. It would involve establishing or strengthening national export controls as well as improving international cooperation to identify and interdict shipments.

Another aspect, "nuclear security culture," describes personnel attitudes toward the importance of nuclear security practices in their daily work. This is known as the "human factor" and recognizes that technology-based physical protection measures are only as effective as the people who are running them. The "insider threat" at nuclear facilities is a worker's knowledge of facility practices that could be used to aid terrorists or smugglers in obtaining material through diversion.

IAEA Definitions of Nuclear Security

Nuclear Security: The prevention and detection of, and response to, theft, sabotage, unauthorized access, illegal transfer or other malicious acts involving nuclear or other radioactive substances or their associated facilities. It should be noted that "nuclear security" includes "physical protection," as that term can be understood from consideration of the Physical Protection Objectives and Fundamental Principles, the CPPNM and the Amendment to the CPPNM.

Nuclear Security Culture: The assembly of characteristics, attitudes and behavior of individuals, organizations and institutions which serves as a means to support and enhance nuclear security.

Source: *Nuclear Security Culture Implementing Guide*, IAEA Nuclear Security Series No. 7, 2008, http://www-pub.iaea.org/MTCD/publications/PDF/Pub1347_web.pdf.

Challenges to Achieving the Four-Year Goal

The four-year goal set out by President Obama of securing "all vulnerable" nuclear materials around the world raises a number of questions, especially what is meant by vulnerable and what is an acceptable definition of "secure." Senator Lugar has defined nuclear security as "a satisfactory level of accountability, transparency, and safety."[29] The highest priority for the United States is to secure weapons-usable material (e.g., that which can be used directly in a nuclear explosive device). This material could be in military fissile material stockpiles or in the civilian fuel cycle. U.S. government efforts will likely start with accelerated activities to secure these materials (see "Funding for Nuclear Security Programs").

One potential obstacle to progress is the sheer volume and wide geographic distribution of the material to be secured. The International Panel on Fissile Material estimates that there are 1,600 tons of HEU and 500 tons of separated plutonium in stocks worldwide.[30] The scope of the problem underlines the Obama Administration's approach that the four-year goal cannot be met by U.S. assistance programs alone, but requires all states to examine their own nuclear security practices and commit their own resources to improving nuclear security.

A challenge to measuring success in reaching the four-year goal will be to establish a baseline accounting of current nuclear material holdings and to improve transparency about current nuclear security practices. To this end, the 2006 National Security Presidential Directive 48 (NSPD-48/HSPD-17) established the Nuclear Materials Information Program (NMIP). NMIP is

---

[29] The Lugar Doctrine states, "The United States will use all of its military, diplomatic and economic power—without question—to ensure that life threatening weapons of mass destruction everywhere are accounted, contained and hopefully destroyed." Some analysts assert this should apply to weapons-usable nuclear material as well as weapons. Press Release, December 6, 2001, http://lugar.senate.gov/bio/doctrine.cfm.

[30] http://www.fissilematerials.org/ipfm/pages_us_en/disarmament/dispositionofpuandheu/dispositionofpuandheu.php.

an interagency effort managed by DOE to "consolidate information from all sources pertaining to worldwide nuclear materials holdings and their security status into an integrated and continuously updated information management system."[31] From open sources, it is not clear that this data collection is complete at this time, or to what extent this inventory includes threat assessments. The IAEA has kept inventory of nuclear material at sites under safeguards (declared nuclear material in non-nuclear weapon states party to the NPT). However, for the nuclear weapon states and non-NPT states, there are few data on inventories.

The majority of states in possession of weapons-usable material participated in the 2010 Nuclear Security Summit, with the prominent exceptions of North Korea, Iran, and Belarus. Each of these cases poses a unique challenge. Belarus houses HEU research reactor fuel, but the United States has done security upgrades on the site, and the material is scheduled to be returned to Russia in FY2011.[32] Iran has a small stock of U.S.-origin used HEU research reactor fuel under international safeguards, but Iran is not willing to return the fuel to the United States at this time.[33] North Korea's plutonium stocks are for weapons purposes, and not under international monitoring.

An additional challenge is convincing developed countries to improve nuclear security measures on their own stocks of HEU and plutonium or HEU research reactors. Other countries may also be sensitive about being to transparent in their nuclear security practices, either for commercial or national security reasons. Another point of contention amongst developed nuclear technology holders is the issue of minimizing or eliminating the use of highly enriched uranium in the civilian fuel cycle. Significant progress has been made in recent years on efforts to remove material from a site or convert a facility to using LEU, rather than HEU, fuel. The G-8 countries have agreed to minimize the use of HEU "to the extent possible." However, highly enriched uranium continues to be used in the civilian fuel cycle, for medical isotope production or research reactors, posing a risk of diversion. The Obama Administration has stopped short of calling for a ban on HEU for civilian use. Some analysts have suggested that U.S. leadership is required to get other countries to support this. Others argue that it is more important to secure international cooperation on this issue and that compromise language in the near term is appropriate.[34] A group of nongovernmental representatives called the Fissile Materials Working Group on September 30, 2009, sent a letter to Administration officials urging that the Obama Administration propose a timetable for HEU phase-out in the civilian fuel cycle at the summit.[35]

Another policy challenge for international nuclear security efforts is how to place this set of issues and joint actions in the context of the wider nuclear nonproliferation regime. Due to the timing of the summit—less than one month before the 2010 Review Conference for the Nuclear Non-Proliferation Treaty—some countries, at least initially, were concerned that the summit was meant to overshadow the Review Conference. The NPT Review Conferences traditionally do not

---

[31] Summary available at http://ftp.fas.org/irp/offdocs/nspd/nspd-48.html.

[32] House Appropriations Subcommittee on Energy and Water Development Hearing, March 10, 2010.

[33] The research reactor was converted to LEU use, but approximately 7 kg of used HEU spent fuel is still housed on-site. "Civil HEU Stock Map," Nuclear Threat Initiative website, http://www.nti.org/db/heu/map.html.

[34] Russia, for example, operates HEU-fueled civilian reactors and has not agreed to a phase-out. For a full discussion of the international dimensions, see "International Politics of Civilian HEU Elimination," Nuclear Threat Initiative website, http://nti.org/db/heu/international.html.

[35] http://www.partnershipforglobalsecurity.org/documents/
fissile_material_policy_recommendations_to_the_obama_administration.pdf.

include in-depth discussion of nuclear material security or nuclear terrorism issues. The traditional three pillars of the NPT are nuclear disarmament, nuclear nonproliferation, and nuclear energy. Some states have proposed that in the post-9/11 security environment, nuclear security issues should be a part of NPT discussions. UK Foreign Minister Millibrand proposed that nuclear security become the "fourth pillar" of the NPT.[36] Also, EU nonproliferation representative Annalisa Giannella has said that since the NPT requires states to prevent proliferation, "one can argue that this obligation also implies the obligation to protect nuclear or radiological material."[37]

However, some developing countries have resisted anything that may be perceived as an additional commitment under the NPT until further disarmament steps are taken. The Obama Administration decided to hold a separate summit on this topic perhaps partially due to this resistance, but also to include non-NPT states in the nuclear security summit and highlight the problem of nuclear diversion to terrorists as a distinct problem. According to U.S. officials, this was not meant to undermine in any way the NPT Review Conference, but to provide an opportunity to focus on addressing the problem of nuclear terrorism at the highest political levels.

Domestic Nuclear Security Measures

The steps the United States takes itself may be important in convincing other countries to take action to improve their own nuclear security. The United States has been working to improve its own nuclear security in recent years. Multiple agencies are involved in the effort. The Department of Defense (DOD) is responsible for securing the U.S. nuclear weapons stockpile, while the Department of Energy (DOE) maintains security at the national laboratories and other facilities in the nuclear weapons complex. DOE is also working to convert the last of the civilian HEU-fueled research reactors in the United States, and has recovered unwanted or excess high-priority radioactive sources in the United States. DOE has completed the conversion of 17 U.S. university HEU-fueled research reactors. Two remaining HEU-fueled university research reactors at the Massachusetts Institute of Technology (MITR) and the University of Missouri (MURR) both require a new higher-density LEU fuel, currently under development.[38]

DOE is also consolidating weapons-usable material within the weapons complex to lessen security risks. In order to improve security over the stocks at U.S. sites with special nuclear material (SNM),[39] the NNSA has been working since October 2006 to consolidate SNM at five sites by 2012, and "significantly reduce square footage at those sites by 2017."[40] The five sites are Los Alamos National Laboratory, the Nevada Test Site, the Savannah River Site, Y-12 Security Complex, and the Idaho National Laboratory. Work on this is ongoing. For example, Los Alamos National Laboratory has removed two-thirds of its SNM requiring the highest levels of protection. Lawrence Livermore National Laboratory announced the removal of 90% of its SNM in September 2011.[41] The Y-12 nuclear complex has concentrated the majority of its SNM stocks at

---

[36] *Road to 2010*, http://www.cabinetoffice.gov.uk/media/224864/roadto2010.pdf.

[37] Daniel Horner, "Nuclear Security Summit Planned for March," *Arms Control Today*, September 2009.

[38] http://nnsa.energy.gov/news/2615 htm.

[39] "Special Nuclear Material" includes highly enriched uranium and plutonium, http://www nrc.gov/materials/sp-nucmaterials html.

[40] See, for example, "NNSA Ships Additional Special Nuclear Material from Lawrence Livermore National Laboratory as part of De-Inventory Project," NNSA Press Release, September 30, 2009, http://nnsa.energy.gov/2628.htm.

[41] "NNSA Ships Additional Material From LLNL," NNSA Press Release, September 1, 2011, http://nnsa.energy.gov/
(continued...)

---

the HEU Materials Facility.[42] The Uranium Processing Facility, to be built in the next decade, is to blend down the remainder of the HEU stocks at Y-12.

The Nuclear Regulatory Commission (NRC) is responsible for security standards at civilian sites. After the 9/11 attacks, security measures at nuclear power plants were improved.[43] The Energy Policy Act of 2005 (P.L. 109-58) mandated that the NRC revise its "Design Based Threat," which specifies the maximum severity of potential attacks that a nuclear plant's security force must be able to repel. This act also required more extensive security checks for personnel at a broad range of nuclear facilities.

U.S. Customs and Border Protection, under the Department of Homeland Security (DHS), uses handheld and portal-based radiation monitors to detect nuclear materials entering the United States.[44] The DHS Science and Technology Directorate conducts research and development to improve radiation detection portals.[45]

Multilateral Efforts to Improve Nuclear Security

One challenge for improving nuclear security around the world has been diverse threat perceptions and varying definitions of nuclear security. For some countries, like the United States, policy makers view the threat of nuclear terrorism as urgent, whereas other countries may see the threat as remote, with trans-shipment of nuclear materials through their territory being of greatest concern. The IAEA document, *The Physical Protection of Nuclear Material and Facilities* (IAEA INFCIRC/225), includes voluntary guidelines meant to strengthen a country's system for nuclear material control. They provide suggested requirements for physical protection against unauthorized diversion or sabotage during use, storage, or transport. It was last amended in 1999, and discussions are underway at the IAEA on how to amend and strengthen these guidelines.

The Convention on the Physical Protection of Nuclear Material and its Amendment is now the most complete legally binding international instrument governing the physical security of nuclear materials, but its adherence is not universal. A 2005 Protocol strengthening the convention will not enter into force until two-thirds of the convention parties have adopted it, a process which could take many more years. The summit called for universality of the Convention and early entry into force of this Amendment.

The IAEA and Nuclear Security

The IAEA is the most prominent international body that promotes nuclear security, and summit documents endorsed its activities and called for a strengthening of the IAEA's role.[46] Over the

---

(...continued)

mediaroom/pressreleases/materiallnl83111.

[42] "NNSA, Y-12 Complete Transfer of Highly Enriched Uranium Ahead of Schedule." NNSA Press Release, August 23, 2011, http://nnsa.energy.gov/mediaroom/pressreleases/transferheumf82311.

[43] See CRS Report RL34331, *Nuclear Power Plant Security and Vulnerabilities*, by Mark Holt and Anthony Andrews.

[44] See CRS Report R40154, *Detection of Nuclear Weapons and Materials: Science, Technologies, Observations*, by Jonathan Medalia.

[45] See CRS Report RL34574, *The Global Nuclear Detection Architecture: Issues for Congress*, by Dana A. Shea.

[46] Note that while India, Israel, and Pakistan are not signatories of the Non-Proliferation Treaty, they are members of (continued...)

years, IAEA member states have adopted voluntary guidelines for nuclear and radiological material security through INFCIRC/225, the Code of Conduct on the Safety and Security of Radioactive Sources, and Guidance on the Import and Export of Radioactive Sources (INFCIRC/663). The fifth revision of INFCIRC/225 was completed in early 2011. The IAEA has routinely assisted countries with improving their nuclear security practices since the 1970s. IAEA safeguards (INFCIRC/153) agreements require that a country have an effective State System of Accountancy and Control (SSAC) for nuclear material.

Just as the focus on nuclear safety drastically increased following the Chernobyl accident, the IAEA's role in nuclear security activities increased following the September 11, 2001, terrorist attacks—which spurred the creation of a distinct Nuclear Security Program at the IAEA.[47] A Nuclear Security Plan was adopted by the IAEA General Conference for 2006-2009 and recently for the period 2010-2013. The second plan emphasizes sustainability of nuclear security practices and training. The IAEA Nuclear Security Program has developed a series of guides on nuclear security topics, and provides in-country assessments and training. The International Physical Protection Advisory Service (IPPAS), for example, provides IAEA member states with confidential expert advice on how to strengthen their physical protection measures and comply with international guidelines. This could include legislation, regulations, licensing, and measures at the facility level. The Nuclear Security Program also works to recover lost radioactive source materials and tracks nuclear trafficking incidents.

The United States provides funds to the Nuclear Security Fund (NSF), an extrabudgetary voluntary fund that supports these activities. The NSF annual budget is approximately $33 million. Starting in 2009, a small portion of the Nuclear Security operating costs is part of the general IAEA budget, but the majority of funds are dependent on voluntary contributions. The United States has supported increasing the portion of funds for the NSF in the IAEA regular budget. The United States dedicated $7 million of its FY2011 voluntary contribution and $8 million in FY2012 to the NSF. Both the Bush and Obama Administrations encouraged strengthening the IAEA's nuclear security activities.

Informal Initiatives and Nonproliferation Assistance

In addition to multilateral treaties and guidelines, a number of initiatives were developed in the past decade to address a wide range of approaches with the goal of gaining broader participation. These approaches include nonproliferation assistance and training programs, joint law enforcement activities, interdiction coordination, and general sharing of best practices. These programs aim to better coordinate governmental efforts to prevent nuclear terrorism—including better coordination within a government at the interagency level and between countries. These efforts are detailed in **Appendix A**, and include the Global Initiative to Combat Nuclear Terrorism, the G-8 Global Partnership, and the Proliferation Security Initiative.

The United States provides extensive aid to foreign countries to secure or remove nuclear materials. These programs, which span several agencies, are detailed in **Appendix B**. Funding for these programs is discussed in the section "Funding for Nuclear Security Programs."

(...continued)

the IAEA.

[47] For more information see IAEA Nuclear Security website, http://www-ns.iaea.org/security/default.htm.

Role of Nongovernmental Organizations and Industry

Nongovernmental organizations play a very active role in recommending ways to address the nuclear terrorism threat and in pointing out gaps in governmental efforts. For the most part, nongovernmental voices on this subject urge more funds and faster governmental action on nuclear material security, and have done so for the past decade or more.[48] Others also have published extensive analysis, particularly on the subject of eliminating HEU from the civilian fuel cycle.[49] A Fissile Material Working Group was formed by a coalition of nongovernmental organizations in advance of the Nuclear Security Summit to jointly recommend courses of action. This group organized a nongovernmental nuclear security summit on April 12, 2010, and subsequent meetings to discuss civil society's contribution to the nuclear security agenda.[50] Skeptical nongovernmental voices tend to criticize the Obama Administration's nuclear weapons policies more generally (including the START treaty and Nuclear Posture Review).[51] While all appear to agree that it is necessary to prevent nuclear terrorism, some would argue that more policy emphasis should be put on counterproliferation initiatives rather than international agreements.

Medical organizations in several countries have expressed interest in halting production of medical isotopes with use of HEU. In May 2008, for example, the Malaysian Medical Association unanimously passed a resolution titled "Eliminating Highly Enriched Uranium from Radiopharmaceutical Production."

Industry associations are also working to promote nuclear security. For example, the World Institute of Nuclear Security (WINS) is an industry-oriented organization that brings together nuclear plant operators to exchange best practices.[52] Industry representatives met following the 2010 summit to discuss how industry can improve nuclear security.

Considerations and Options for Congress

Legislation in the 112th Congress

The House and Senate Judiciary Committees are considering implementing legislation for the Nuclear Terrorism Convention, CPPNM Amendment, 2005 SUA Protocols.[53] The Senate

---

[48] *Securing the Bomb*, http://www nti.org/e_research/cnwm/overview/cnwm_home.asp.

[49] See, for example, the July 2008 edition of *Nonproliferation Review* devoted to the global elimination of highly enriched uranium at http://cns miis.edu/npr/152toc htm.

[50] For a list of member organizations, see http://fmwg.presstools.org/about The FMWG sent a letter to Obama Administration officials in September 2009 recommending Summit outcomes: http://fmwg.presstools.org/node/34505. The group's recommendations for the 2012 Seoul Summit available at http://www fissilematerialsworkinggroup.org/ FMWGRecommendationsRpt1912.pdf.

[51] See, for example, remarks at the "Questioning Obama's Nuclear Agenda Conservative Counter Summit," Heritage Foundation, April 6, 2010, http://www heritage.org/Events/2010/04/Questioning-Obamas-Nuclear-Agenda.

[52] For more information, see http://www.wins.org/.

[53] Protocol of 2005 to the Convention for the Suppression of Unlawful Acts against the Safety of Maritime Navigation, (continued...)

---

approved resolutions of advice and consent to ratification for these agreements in September 2008 (Treaty documents 110-4, 110-6, 110-8). Implementing legislation is required before the United States can ratify them. The Bush Administration sent draft legislation to the committee in 2008, and the Obama Administration first sent draft legislation to the committee in late March 2010, but legislation was not introduced. Draft legislation was submitted to the 112th Congress on the first anniversary of the Nuclear Security Summit, April 13, 2011. The White House press release said that the proposed legislation would "update the U.S. Criminal Code to strengthen our ability to fully investigate and prosecute acts of nuclear terrorism."[54] The House Judiciary Committee held a hearing on the legislation on October 5, 2011.

Senator Jeff Bingaman introduced the American Medical Isotopes Production Act of 2011 (S. 99) in January 2011. Senator Lisa Murkowski co-sponsors the bill. S. 99 was reported out of the Senate Committee on Energy and Natural Resources on April 12, 2011, and passed by the full Senate on November 17, 2011 (S.Rept. 112-17). It was referred to the House Committee on Science, Space and Technology, Subcommittee on Energy and the Environment. The bill seeks to promote the domestic (U.S.) production of molybdenum-99 for medical isotope production, and to condition and phase out the export of HEU for the production of medical isotopes within seven years after enactment. A phase-out of U.S. export of HEU for medical isotope production could strengthen U.S. calls for other countries to also eventually eliminate the use of HEU for civilian purposes.[55]

The House Foreign Affairs Committee approved H.R. 1280 sponsored by Committee Chairman Ileana Ros-Lehtinen and five co-sponsors on April 14, 2011. This bill would amend provisions of the Atomic Energy Act relevant to bilateral nuclear cooperation agreements. Among other changes to the nonproliferation requirements for cooperation,[56] the bill would require partner states to be in full compliance with the Convention on the Physical Protection of Nuclear Material and the United Nations International Convention for the Suppression of Acts of Nuclear Terrorism.

Legislation in the 111th Congress

The Nuclear Forensics and Attribution Act (P.L. 111-140), originally introduced by Representative Schiff, became law in February 2010. It expresses the sense of Congress that the President should pursue agreements to establish an international framework for nuclear forensics analysis on confiscated nuclear material and develop protocols for data exchange. It also amends the Homeland Security Act of 2002 to establish a National Technical Nuclear Forensics Center within the Domestic Nuclear Detection Office.

(...continued)

and the Protocol of 2005 to the Protocol for the Suppression of Unlawful Acts against the Safety of Fixed Platforms Located on the Continental Shelf.

[54] "Statement of the Press Secretary on the Submission of Legislation Required for Four Key Nuclear Security Treaties," White House Press Release, April 13, 2011, http://m.whitehouse.gov/the-press-office/2011/04/13/statement-press-secretary-submission-legislation-required-four-key-nucle.

[55] The House passed a similar bill in the 111th Congress—the American Medical Isotopes Production Act of 2010 (H.R. 3276) in November 2009. It was originally introduced by Representative Markey. It was reported out of the Senate Committee on Energy and Natural Resources with amendments in January 2010.

[56] For a more detailed discussion, see CRS Report RS22937, *Nuclear Cooperation with Other Countries: A Primer*, by Paul K. Kerr and Mary Beth Nikitin.

Senator Casey and Representative Schiff introduced the Nuclear Trafficking Prevention Act (S. 1464, H.R. 3244) in July 2009. The bill would amend the federal criminal code to prohibit the transfer of a nuclear weapon or device, or of nuclear material or sensitive nuclear technology, to any foreign terrorist organization or any other person engaged in terrorist activities. It would grant extraterritorial jurisdiction to prosecute violations and impose a fine and minimum prison term of 25 years for violations (life imprisonment for violations resulting in death). It also says the transfer of a nuclear weapon or device or of nuclear material or technology for terrorist purposes should be a crime against humanity and should be punished under customary international criminal law.

Senator Akaka introduced the Strengthening the Oversight of Nuclear Nonproliferation Act of 2009 (S. 1931). This act would require the President's Coordinator for the Prevention of Weapons of Mass Destruction Proliferation and Terrorism to report to the appropriate congressional committees (1) annually regarding the Commission on the Prevention of Weapons of Mass Destruction Proliferation and Terrorism's findings concerning U.S. nuclear nonproliferation efforts, and (2) regarding U.S. cooperative efforts with the International Atomic Energy Agency (IAEA) on nuclear nonproliferation. The commission made several recommendations related to preventing nuclear terrorism.

Funding for Nuclear Security Programs

In its annual appropriations, Congress decides on funding for U.S. domestic and international programs focused on nuclear material security and nuclear terrorism prevention. As detailed in **Appendix B**, these programs are primarily implemented by the Departments of Defense, Energy, State, and Homeland Security. The intelligence community also clearly plays a key role in analyzing nuclear terrorism threats and illicit trafficking issues.

The Obama Administration's FY2011, FY2012, and FY2013 congressional budget requests proposed overall increases in funding for nuclear security-related accounts, with the stated purpose of ramping up programs to meet the President's four-year goal. These budget increases are primarily visible in the DOE NNSA Defense Nonproliferation programs. Critics have pointed out that some of the increases are due to expensive construction projects related to U.S. fissile material disposition, and programs for international material security have struggled to maintain (or have decreased) funding levels. **Appendix C** details changes in DOE nonproliferation programs since FY2007. The DOD, State Department, and DHS programs have for the most part reprogrammed money from other parts of their nonproliferation or threat-reduction funds to programs that would contribute to global nuclear security goals. The major issues during the past few years of budget deliberations are summarized below.

The FY2011 Budget Debate

Congress struggled to pass an appropriations bills for FY2011, and instead funded the federal government through a series of continuing resolutions, ending with appropriations for the full fiscal year passed on April 15, 2011 (P.L. 112-10). This bill avoided a government shut-down, which might have had an impact on the pace of programs to secure and remove nuclear materials overseas.

The nuclear security-related assistance programs were at risk of significant budget cuts throughout this process, particularly the Department of Energy's defense nuclear nonproliferation accounts. These programs are authorized by Armed Services committees but are funded through the Energy and Water Appropriations bill. Cuts were proposed by House leadership to all non-defense-related programs. Until late March, it appeared that the NNSA budget was not being considered as a defense activity, perhaps due to its appropriations under the Energy and Water bill. All 16 members of the House Armed Services Committee Strategic Forces Subcommittee sent a letter on March 23, 2011, to Budget Committee Chairman Paul Ryan urging full funding of the NNSA programs as national security programs. In the end, P.L. 112-10 funded nuclear security programs at a greater level than was expected, although specific breakdowns of how the agencies will distribute the money at the program level are not yet available. FY2011 funding for NNSA's defense nuclear nonproliferation is approximately $2.3 billion, compared with the FY2011 request of nearly $2.7 billion, and the FY2010 appropriation of $2.1 billion. Anne Harrington, who directs the NNSA nonproliferation programs, has said that work has continued on schedule despite the uncertain funding levels.[57]

Nuclear security-related DOD programs were funded at request and have changed little in total funding in the past several years, although funding between subprograms has shifted.[58] Several new efforts were proposed in the nuclear security area under the Cooperative Threat Reduction (CTR) program. In its FY2011 budget request, the DOD proposed $74 million for a new initiative under CTR to help fulfill the four-year goal. The Global Nuclear Lockdown (GNL) would include establishing regional centers of excellence for nuclear security around the world. They are meant to "assess equipment and manpower, provide material security training, and demonstrate enhanced security procedures and processes."[59] Sections 1303 and 1304 of the FY2011 National Defense Authorization Act (P.L. 111-383) require the DOD and DOE to report to Congress in advance of any disbursements of funds over $500,000 for a center of excellence outside the former Soviet Union. They also require a separate report detailing activities with China.

The State Department faced budget cuts across the board, and it is not yet clear how the funding will be disbursed to specific nonproliferation programs, but nuclear security-related programs will likely continue as planned. The Obama Administration has increased funding to these programs.

The FY2012 Budget Request

The Obama Administration continued to increase its requests for funding for nuclear security-related programs in the FY2012 budget request. NNSA Administrator Thomas D'Agostino has described the FY2012 budget request as providing "the resources required to meet commitments secured during the 2010 Nuclear Security Summit, including removing all remaining highly enriched uranium (HEU) from Belarus, Ukraine, and Mexico and working with the Defense Department to implement nuclear security Centers of Excellence in China and India."[60]

Much of the budget debate for FY2012 appropriations continues to be driven by proposals from the House leadership. Budget Committee Chairman Ryan's "budget blueprint" did not address

---

[57] *Nuclear Weapons & Materials Monitor*, April 22, 2011, p. 3.

[58] See CRS Report RL31957, *Nonproliferation and Threat Reduction Assistance: U.S. Programs in the Former Soviet Union*, by Amy F. Woolf.

[59] FY2011 Budget Estimate, Cooperative Threat Reduction Program, http://comptroller.defense.gov/defbudget/fy2011/budget_justification/pdfs/01_Operation_and_Maintenance/O_M_VOL_1_PARTS/CTR_FY11.pdf.

[60] "FY2012 Budget Request Includes Critical Investment in Nuclear Security Enterprise," Department of Energy Press Conference February 14, 2011, http://nnsa.energy.gov/mediaroom/pressreleases/fy12budget21411.

nonproliferation or nuclear security funding specifically, but did promise full funding for the U.S. nuclear weapons stockpile-related programs.[61]

FY2012 Department of Defense Request

The Defense Threat Reduction Agency's (DTRA's) Cooperative Threat Reduction (CTR) program requested $121,143,000 for the Global Nuclear Security account for FY2012. The Global Nuclear Security account was reduced by $45,877,000 from the FY2011 request due to the phasing out of work in Kazakhstan and reduced efforts in Russia. The Nuclear Weapons Transportation Security program for Russia was zeroed out in the FY2012 proposal because work was completed on rail car procurement efforts in Russia.

Other CTR programs also contribute to nuclear security, such as Proliferation Prevention, which addresses illicit trafficking, and Threat Reduction Engagement for work outside the former Soviet Union. Proliferation Prevention works to build the capacity of partner countries to detect and interdict illicit transfers of WMD-related materials or technology across land borders or at seaports. DTRA's work focuses on Ukraine's borders with Moldova and Russia. This program is coordinated with the DOE's Second Line of Defense program, State Department's EXBS program, and DOD's International Counterproliferation Program.

FY2012 Department of Energy Request

For NNSA's defense nuclear nonproliferation accounts, the Administration requested $2.5 billion in FY2012 and $14.2 billion over the next five years (compared with $2.3 billion in FY2011). Over the years, Congress has often added funds, both during the regular appropriations process and the supplemental appropriations process, to many of the programs funded in this budget. Generally, these additions indicate congressional support for the programs that are designed to enhance security at facilities that house nuclear weapons and materials, those that are designed to secure borders and ports against the transport of nuclear materials and weapons, and those that are part of the global effort to secure and remove vulnerable nuclear materials. The higher level of the FY2011 request may have partially been to encourage Congress to fund these programs through the regular budget process rather than through supplemental appropriations. The FY2012 request is more modest than in FY2011, most likely due to overall budget pressure.

FY2012 Department of State Request

State Department programs that address nuclear material security are part of programs that address all weapons of mass destruction proliferation or terrorism. The total level of funding for the Nonproliferation Programs under the State Department's Nonproliferation, Antiterrorism, Demining and Related Programs (NADR) account remains fairly constant in the FY2012 request at $293,829,000 (compared with $295 million in FY2010 and FY2011). There are changes at the subprogram level: a $45 million reduction in the Nonproliferation Disarmament Fund, and notable increases in the Export Control and Related Border Security (EXBS) assistance and in the Weapons of Mass Destruction Terrorism accounts. A new contribution of $1.5 million to the U.N.

---

[61] Martin Matishak, "GOP Budget Plan Maintains Nuclear Modernization Funds," April 6, 2011, *National Journal On-Line*, http://www.nationaljournal.com/nationalsecurity/gop-budget-plan-maintains-nuclear-modernization-funds-20110406?print=true.

Security Council Resolution 1540 Trust Fund is aimed at helping foreign countries' capacity to prevent illicit nuclear (and other WMD) trafficking.

FY2012 Authorizations and Appropriations

Programs that address nuclear security around the world are based primarily in the Department of Energy's Defense Nuclear Nonproliferation account under the NNSA; the Department of Defense's Cooperative Threat Reduction Program; and the State Department's Nonproliferation, Antiterrorism and Demining and Related programs. The DOE's Defense Nuclear Nonproliferation account is authorized by the Armed Services Committees and funds are appropriated by the Energy and Water Appropriations Subcommittees.

FY2012 Defense Authorization

The House adopted its version of the FY2012 National Defense Authorization Act on May 26, 2011 (H.R. 1540), fully funding both the requests for the Department of Defense CTR programs and the Department of Energy's Defense Nuclear Nonproliferation (H.Rept. 112-78). An additional $20 million was added for GTRI work by an amendment introduced by Representative Loretta Sanchez, ranking Member of the HASC Strategic Forces Subcommittee. The House report raised concerns about the $26 million from DOE funds proposed for the Center for Excellence in China. The committee questioned the necessity of paying for best practices training in a country that is "economically advanced" and raised questions over proliferation from China. H.R. 1540, Section 2112, requires that no more than $7 million may be obligated or expended until required reports are submitted to the House and Senate Armed Services Committees. The reports by the Department of Energy in consultation with the Department of Defense are a review of the "existing capacity of the People's Republic of China to develop and implement best practices training for nuclear security," and a report on "the extent to which the training and relationship-building activities planned for the United States-China Center of Excellence on Nuclear Security could contribute to improving China's historical patterns with respect to the proliferation of weapons of mass destruction and missiles."

The Senate version of the Defense Authorization Act (S. 1253) was approved by the Senate Armed Services Committee on June 17, 2011 (S.Rept. 112-26). The committee recommended full funding (at request, or $508.2 million) of DOD's Cooperative Threat Reduction program. The committee recommended $2.5 billion for DOE/NNSA Defense Nuclear Nonproliferation, $2.8 million below the budget request. The committee's report emphasized the importance of coordination between the Departments of Energy and Defense on this work:

> The committee also supports the effort to secure the most vulnerable nuclear material in 4 years, but recognizes that this is a significant challenge that will require close interagency cooperation to be fully successful. The committee notes that the Department of Defense and the Department of Energy, National Nuclear Security Administration, have a long and productive history of cooperation in threat reduction programs, and urge them to continue this close collaboration in the accelerated program.

FY2012 Energy and Water Appropriations

The House passed the FY2012 Energy and Water Appropriations Act on July 15, 2011 (H.R. 2354). The Department of Energy's Defense Nuclear Nonproliferation Account was funded at

$2.091 billion, a reduction of $468 million below the Administration's FY2012 request and $182 million below FY2011 appropriations (see **Appendix C**). House appropriators in committee reduced funding levels for several defense nuclear nonproliferation accounts—the fissile material disposition account, Global Threat Reduction Initiative (research reactor conversion and domestic radiological program), Second Line of Defense, International Nuclear Materials Protection and Control (INMPC), and Nonproliferation and Verification Research and Development accounts (H.Rept. 112-118). The committee's report says that "the recommendation fully supports the Administration's four year goal to secure vulnerable nuclear material worldwide as an urgent national security need and priority of the Committee." At the same time, the committee report says that some program cuts were made due to inefficiencies or "overly optimistic" estimates about what would be accomplished in the coming year. A successful amendment on the House floor by Representatives Fortenberry, Sanchez, Garamendi, and Larsen restored $35 million of the $70 million in proposed cuts to the GTRI research reactor conversion program. In a floor statement Representative Loretta Sanchez said that restoration of the funding would "prevent delays of at least one year to Highly Enriched Uranium reactor conversions in Poland, Kazakhstan, Uzbekistan, Ghana and Nigeria." That program is considered a key component of the effort to secure nuclear materials worldwide.

The Senate Appropriations Committee on September 7 approved funding the DOE's Defense Nuclear Nonproliferation Account at $2.383 billion, a reduction of $167 million below the Administration's FY2012 request and $110 million above FY2011 appropriations. In report language (S.Rept. 112-75), the committee praised NNSA's progress on nuclear security activities:

> The Committee commends NNSA for making significant progress in meeting the goal of securing all vulnerable nuclear materials within 4 years. In 2009, the Congressional Commission on the Strategic Posture of the United States found that "the surest way to prevent nuclear terrorism is to deny terrorist acquisition of nuclear weapons or fissile materials ... An accelerated campaign to close or secure the world's most vulnerable nuclear sites as quickly as possible should be a top national priority." To that end, since April 2009, when President Obama announced the 4-year goal, NNSA has removed over 960 kilograms of highly enriched uranium—enough material for 38 nuclear weapons. NNSA has also removed all highly enriched uranium from six countries. One of these countries was Libya. Given the recent unrest in Libya, the presence of this dangerous nuclear material in an unstable part of the world would have increased the risk of nuclear terrorism. Removing highly enriched uranium from six countries in 2 years is much faster than one country a year NNSA has averaged in the last 13 years. Further, NNSA has completed security upgrades at 32 additional buildings in Russia containing weapons usable materials. The Committee encourages NNSA to continue its accelerated efforts to secure vulnerable nuclear materials.

FY2012 Department of State Appropriations

The State Department request for Nonproliferation programs at $293,829,000 under the NADR account was fully funded. The Senate Committee on Appropriations (S.Rept. 112-85) and House Committee on Appropriations (H.Rept. 112-331) both recommended funding at the requested levels, specifying $30 million be available for the Nonproliferation and Disarmament Fund, and encouraging nonproliferation work in Libya as needed.

The FY2013 Budget Request

The Obama Administration submitted its FY2013 budget requests to Congress in early February. The requests related to the international nuclear material security programs are summarized below for the Departments of Defense, Energy, and State. Some non-governmental experts have issued statements critical of the DOE budget proposal in particular, saying that the reduced funding levels are contrary to the stated goals of the Nuclear Security Summit process.[62] The Administration's budget requests and official statements appear to set out a case saying that the reduced funding is reflective of the accomplishment of many of the Administration's key nuclear security goals.[63] Some reductions may also reflect overall pressure to reduce spending under the Budget Control Act. This debate is likely to be detailed in authorization and appropriations hearings this spring.

FY2013 Department of Defense Request

The Defense Threat Reduction Agency's (DTRA's) Cooperative Threat Reduction (CTR) program requested $99,789,000 for its Global Nuclear Security (GNS) account for FY2013. The GNS account was reduced from a $121,143,000 request and appropriation in FY2012. According to the FY2013 congressional budget justification, this decrease is due to the completion of fissile material security efforts in Kazakhstan and reduced efforts in Russia as responsibilities for security upgrades are transferred to the Russian Ministry of Defense. FY2013 efforts are to include continued support and training for the Russian Ministry of Defense to sustain warhead security upgrades, transportation of 48 trainloads of deactivated Russian warheads (1,000 to 1,500) to secure storage, support for the development of nuclear security centers of excellence, and assistance in the transportation of spent nuclear fuel as part of global clean-out efforts as needed. As detailed above and in **Appendix B**, other DOD CTR programs that address WMD proliferation also contribute to nuclear security goals.

FY2013 Department of Energy Request

The Administration requested $2.46 billion for NNSA's defense nuclear nonproliferation accounts in FY2013. This is an increase over the appropriated amount ($2.295 billion), but roughly equivalent to the Administration's FY2012 request. The budget request says that the amounts reflect "completion of accelerated efforts to secure vulnerable nuclear materials within four years, the President's stated timeframe." For details, see **Table C-1**.

Proposed budget increases are found in the Fissile Material Disposition funding line, for U.S. disposition of excess plutonium stocks through construction of a MOX facility in Savannah River. Another notable item was the addition of $150 million in RD&D funding for USEC's American Centrifuge enrichment technology in the Nonproliferation and Verification account. The inclusion of this "one-time" line item in the nonproliferation part of DOE's budget rather than in nuclear energy may indicate DOE will emphasize national security reasons for funding the program. However, national security justifications are a subject of debate. Some analysts worry that adding this item to the DNN account is causing unnecessary cuts to nuclear and radiological security efforts.

---

[62] "Obama Administration Cuts Vital Programs Combating Nuclear Terrorism," Fissile Materials Working Group Press Release, February 14, 2012, http://www.fissilematerialsworkinggroup.org/news.cfm?action=article&page=0&id=9c4eb174-8b56-47c2-99f8-acf5ff5f32b5.

[63] Kenneth Fletcher, "Nonproliferation Request Reflects NNSA'sShifting Priorities for FY2013," *Nuclear Weapons & Materials Monitor*, February 14, 2012.

The sharpest proposed budget decreases are found in the International Nuclear Materials Protection and Cooperation (INMP&C) program. The INMP&C program decreases reflect the conclusion of key nuclear security projects in Russia that will be administered by the Russian Ministry of Defense at the end of FY2012. The request also includes a major reduction for the Second Line of Defense program. According to the request, this reflects "the completion of installation of detection equipment at a cumulative 496 SLD sites, including 45 Megaports." House appropriators in FY2012 report language recommended that NNSA revisit the goals and measures of effectiveness for this program.[64]

The Global Threat Reduction Initiative (GTRI) justification shows that the nearly $32 million proposed overall decrease for GTRI activities is mainly due to a decrease in the Nuclear and Radiological Materials Removal account. While the Gap Nuclear Material Removal program projects an increase, reductions to the Russian-Origin and U.S.-Origin Nuclear Material Programs together would total a $49 million decrease. The budget request says this is "consistent with the four-year plan." Some activities may have long timelines for completion and were therefore funded in FY2012. According to the NNSA budget request, additional reactor conversions and HEU removals are being planned through 2017. Congress may wish to consider how funding for these programs impacts timelines for removal and conversion.

FY2013 Department of State Request

State Department programs that address nuclear material security are part of programs that address all weapons of mass destruction proliferation or terrorism. The total level of funding for the Nonproliferation Programs under the State Department's Nonproliferation, Antiterrorism, Demining and Related Programs (NADR) account decreased by almost $12.5 million. Decreases in funding are primarily for the Export Control and Related Border Security (EXBS) and Global Threat Reduction (GTR) accounts (although biosecurity funding within GTR was increased). A contribution of $1.35 million (compared to $1.5 million in FY2012) to the U.N. Security Council Resolution 1540 Trust Fund is aimed at helping foreign countries' capacity to prevent illicit nuclear (and other WMD) trafficking.

FY2013 Authorizations and Appropriations

Congress is currently considering the Administration's budget request through hearings and briefings. It also continues to conduct oversight of management issues as part of this process. A

---

[64] "With over $1,500,000,000 already spent to install radiation detectors around the world, the Committee is concerned that there are not adequate performance measures to gauge the effectiveness of this effort. The primary performance measure used by the NNSA is the number of detectors installed, but the true effectiveness of these detectors in preventing proliferation is largely dependent on how well individual countries employ these capabilities in their security operations. The Committee directs the NNSA to perform a study, either through survey or inspection, on how individual countries are employing these capabilities after they have been installed. The study should attempt to determine whether the equipment is being effectively employed and adequately maintained, including whether a sufficient volume of screening is being performed and whether ongoing training is being conducted by host countries to maintain proficiency. The NNSA should report the results of its study to the Committee which includes an overall assessment by country of the readiness levels to detect nuclear and radiological materials, as determined by the effectiveness of ongoing activities after the equipment has been installed. The report should also identify by country equipment that will continue to be maintained by the NNSA and the associated ongoing costs." House Energy and Water Appropriations Committee, H.Rept. 112-118, June 24, 2011.

hearing on "Managing Interagency Nuclear Nonproliferation Efforts: Are We Effectively Securing Nuclear Materials Around the World?" will be held by Senate Homeland Security and Governmental Affairs Subcommittee on Oversight of Government Management, the Federal Workforce and the District of Columbia on March 14, 2012.

Considerations

It should be noted that looking simply at whether budget amounts are increased or decreased may not provide a full picture of the U.S. commitment to nuclear security. As more nuclear materials are secured or removed in countries open to cooperation, programs will spend more effort on securing agreement from countries resistant to such measures. The summit may have helped open some of these doors, but many countries may still see sensitive materials as a technological asset or may have a more lax attitude toward the threat of material diversion. In addition, in some cases, countries will be more comfortable working with a donor country other than the United States, or with a nongovernmental organization due to sensitivities in the bilateral relationship. Others may choose to address nuclear security programs quietly with the United States or others. This will require U.S. persuasion and diplomacy, which is more difficult to budget. In addition, as cooperative threat reduction work generally shifts from capital intensive projects such as building a material storage site to sustainability and training related work, the funding necessary will likely eventually decrease while the work could still provide significant benefits.

Appendix A. Multilateral Nuclear Security-Related Instruments and Initiatives

U.N. Security Council Resolutions

In September 2009, President Obama chaired a U.N. Security Council Summit that focused on nuclear nonproliferation. The Security Council adopted Resolution 1887, which called on countries to improve their nuclear security and step up efforts to prevent nuclear trafficking.[65] This resolution was unanimously adopted and endorsed President Obama's goal of securing all vulnerable nuclear material within four years.

Previous efforts at the U.N. Security Council have also strengthened the international community's efforts to convince all countries that the threat of nuclear terrorism should be addressed in every country, whether it holds stocks of nuclear (or other WMD) material or not. Resolution 1540 was adopted in April 2004 and requires all states to "criminalize proliferation, enact strict export controls and secure all sensitive materials within their borders." UNSCR 1540 called on states to enforce effective domestic controls over WMD and WMD-related materials in production, use, storage, and transport; to maintain effective border controls; and to

> ### U.N. Security Council Resolution 1887, September 2009
>
> "24. *Calls upon* Member States to share best practices with a view to improved safety standards and nuclear security practices and raise standards of nuclear security to reduce the risk of nuclear terrorism, with the aim of securing all vulnerable nuclear material from such risks within four years;
>
> 25. *Calls upon* all States to manage responsibly and minimize to the greatest extent that is technically and economically feasible the use of highly enriched uranium for civilian purposes, including by working to convert research reactors and radioisotope production processes to the use of low enriched uranium fuels and targets;
>
> 26. *Calls upon* all States to improve their national capabilities to detect, deter, and disrupt illicit trafficking in nuclear materials throughout their territories, and calls upon those States in a position to do so to work to enhance international partnerships and capacity building in this regard;
>
> 27. *Urges* all States to take all appropriate national measures in accordance with their national authorities and legislation, and consistent with international law, to prevent proliferation financing and shipments, to strengthen export controls, to secure sensitive materials, and to control access to intangible transfers of technology."

develop national export and trans-shipment controls over such items, all of which should help interdiction efforts. The resolution did not, however, provide any enforcement authority, nor did it specifically mention interdiction. U.N. Security Council Resolutions 1673 (2006), 1810 (2008) and 1977 (2011) extended the duration of the 1540 Committee. The committee is currently focused on identifying assistance projects for states in need and matching donors to improve these WMD controls. The Obama Administration has proposed extra-budgetary contributions to the U.N. for a Trust Fund to implement 1540-related projects, such as training.

UNSCR 1540 carries the status of a mandatory legal obligation for all U.N. member states, as it was adopted under Chapter VII of the U.N. Charter. In addition, as mentioned above, the Convention's provisions calling for information sharing and cooperation establish a basis to rally international support for efforts such as the Global Initiative to Combat Nuclear Terrorism, the

---

[65] "Historic Summit of Security Council Pledges Support for Progress on Stalled Efforts to End Nuclear Proliferation," SC/9746, September 24, 2009, http://www.un.org/News/Press/docs/2009/sc9746.doc.

U.S.-led Global Threat Reduction Initiative, Proliferation Security Initiative (where intelligence sharing is key), and additional international nuclear security and counterproliferation efforts.

Another relevant resolution, U.N. Security Council Resolution 1373, adopted in September 2001, calls on states to prevent and suppress the financing of terrorism, and to deny terrorists safe haven.

Treaties

A number of international treaties govern the security of nuclear material, but none are universal, and together they make up a patchwork approach to the problem to date.

Convention on the Physical Protection of Nuclear Material and Amendment

The Convention on the Physical Protection of Nuclear Material, adopted in 1987, sets international standards for securing nuclear material in trade and commerce. The Convention established security requirements for the protection of nuclear materials in international transit against terrorism. Parties to the treaty also agree to report shipments to the IAEA. In 2005, the States Parties extended the scope of the Convention to include nuclear material in domestic use, storage, and transport, as well as the protection of nuclear material and facilities from sabotage.

The 2005 Amendment could potentially augment U.S. efforts to cooperate with other countries to prevent nuclear terrorism. Although the treaty itself does not have any enforcement mechanisms for compliance with its provisions, it raises standards for physical protection, defines criminal offenses, and provides a legal basis for cooperation that would bolster several existing international efforts. Criticism of the Amendment has primarily been limited to arguments that it does not go far enough to advance the nonproliferation agenda. Some analysts criticize the Amendment for not covering military stocks of nuclear materials, not including verification measures, and issuing "overly vague" guidelines for physical protection. They argue that the Amendment says only that nuclear facilities and materials should be protected, not specifically how they should be protected.[66]

The new rules will only come into effect once the Amendment has been ratified by two-thirds of the States Parties of the Convention, which could take several years. As of January 2011, only 46 states (out of 142 Convention parties) had ratified the amendment. On September 4, 2007, President Bush submitted the amendment to the Senate for its advice and consent on ratification. The Secretary of State's Letter of Submittal says that once the Amendment enters into force, it will "significantly strengthen" the worldwide physical protection of nuclear material and facilities used for peaceful purposes. In the Letter of Transmittal, President Bush called it "important in the campaign against international nuclear terrorism and nuclear proliferation."

The Senate Committee on Foreign Relations recommended that the Senate give its advice and consent on September 11, 2008. The Senate must approve implementing legislation before the

---

[66] "International Nuclear Security Standards," Nuclear Threat Reduction Campaign, Veterans for America, available at http://www.veteransforamerica.org/wp-content/uploads/2008/01/25-physical-sec-y-standards.pdf. Securing the Bomb 2007, *Nuclear Threat Initiative* website, http://www.nti.org/e_research/securingthebomb07.pdf. George Bunn, "Enforcing International Standards: Protecting Nuclear Materials From Terrorists Post-9/11," *Arms Control Today*, January/February 2007, available at http://www.armscontrol.org/act/2007_01-02/Bunn.asp.

United States deposits its instrument of ratification to the Amendment. The Obama Administration submitted draft implementing legislation for consideration to the Judiciary Committee in April 2011.

Nuclear Terrorism Convention

The U.N. General Assembly adopted the International Convention for the Suppression of Acts of Nuclear Terrorism (also known as the Nuclear Terrorism Convention or NTC) in 2005 after eight years of debating a draft treaty proposed by Russia in 1997. Disputes over the definition of terrorism, omitted in the final version, and over the issue of nuclear weapons use by states, complicated the discussions for many years. After September 11, 2001, states revisited the draft treaty and the necessary compromises were made. The Convention entered into force in July 2007 and had 77 States Parties and 115 signatories as of April 2011. The United States has strongly supported the Convention, and President Bush was the second to sign it (after Russian President Putin) on September 14, 2005. The Senate Committee on Foreign Relations reported the treaty to the full Senate and recommended advice and consent on September 11, 2008. The Senate must approve implementing legislation before the United States deposits its instrument of ratification to the Convention. The Obama Administration submitted draft legislation was submitted to the Judiciary Committee in April 2011.

The Convention defines offenses related to the unlawful possession and use of radioactive or nuclear material or devices, and the use or damage to nuclear facilities. The Convention commits each party to adopt measures in its national law to criminalize these offenses and make them punishable. It covers acts by individuals, not states, and does not govern the actions of armed forces during an armed conflict. The Convention also does not address "the issue of legality of the use or threat of use of nuclear weapons by States." It also commits States Parties to exchange information and cooperate to "detect, prevent, suppress and investigate" those suspected of committing nuclear terrorism, including extraditions.

The NTC could potentially augment U.S. efforts to cooperate with other countries to combat nuclear terrorism. Although the treaty itself does not have any enforcement mechanisms for compliance with its provisions, it could provide a legal basis for cooperation and bolster several existing international efforts. The UNSCR 1540 could provide a vehicle to spur compliance with the NTC.

Other International Initiatives

Global Initiative to Combat Nuclear Terrorism

In July 2006, Russia and the United States announced the creation of the Global Initiative to Combat Nuclear Terrorism before the G-8 Summit in St. Petersburg. This initiative is non-binding, but requires agreement on a statement of principles. Thirteen nations—Australia, Canada, China, France, Germany, Italy, Japan, Kazakhstan, Morocco, Turkey, the United Kingdom, the United States, and Russia—endorsed a Statement of Principles at the Initiative's first meeting in October 2006. The International Atomic Energy Agency (IAEA) and the

European Union (EU) have observer status. As of April 2011, 82 states have agreed to the statement of principles and are Global Initiative partner nations.[67]

U.S. officials have described the Initiative as a "flexible framework" to prevent, detect, and respond to the threat of nuclear terrorism. It is meant to enhance information sharing and build capacity worldwide. The Statement of Principles pledges to improve each nation's ability to secure radioactive and nuclear material, prevent illicit trafficking by improving detection of such material, respond to a terrorist attack, prevent safe haven to potential nuclear terrorists and financial resources, and ensure liability for acts of nuclear terrorism. Participating states share a common goal to improve national capabilities to combat nuclear terrorism by sharing best practices through multinational exercises and expert level meetings. Without dues or a secretariat, actions under the Initiative will take legal guidance from the International Convention on the Suppression of Acts of Nuclear Terrorism, the Convention on the Physical Protection of Nuclear Materials, and U.N. Security Council Resolutions 1540 and 1373. President Obama in an April 2009 speech said that the Global Initiative should be turned into a "durable international institution," but how this would be implemented is not yet clear.

G-8 Global Partnership

The Global Partnership Against the Spread of Weapons and Materials of Mass Destruction was announced by the Group of Eight (G-8) Nations at their 2002 summit. The G-8 members agreed to raise $20 billion over 10 years for nonproliferation-related assistance beginning in Russia, of which the United States committed to providing $10 billion. Since 2002, 12 additional countries and the European Union have joined the G-8 as donors. The Global Partnership countries have recently agreed to extend the Global Partnership to recipients worldwide on a case-by-case basis. Nuclear security and fissile material disposition programs have played a prominent role in Global Partnership programs. Some countries, including the United States, would like the Global Partnership renewed for another 10 years, and would like to see nuclear material security as a key component of future assistance. Thus, the Global Partnership could be a key means for international coordination of funding nuclear security assistance programs. The G-8 decided to continue the Global Partnership past 2012 at their 2011 Summit in Deauville, France. They reaffirmed the goals set out at the 2010 Summit for future Global Partnership activities: nuclear and radiological security, bio-security, scientist engagement, and facilitation of the implementation of U.N. Security Council Resolution 1540.

Proliferation Security Initiative

The Proliferation Security Initiative (PSI) was formed to increase international cooperation in interdicting shipments of weapons of mass destruction (WMD), their delivery systems, and related materials. The initiative was announced by President Bush on May 31, 2003. PSI does not create a new legal framework but aims to use existing national authorities and international law to achieve its goals. Initially, 11 nations signed on to the "Statement of Interdiction Principles" that guides PSI cooperation. As of April 2011, 97 countries have committed formally to the PSI principles, although the extent of participation may vary by country. PSI has no secretariat, but an Operational Experts Group (OEG), made up of 21 PSI participants, coordinates activities.

---

[67] "Partner Nations List," State Department website, http://www.state.gov/t/isn/c37083.htm.

Although WMD interdiction efforts took place with international cooperation before PSI was formed, supporters argue that PSI training exercises and boarding agreements give a structure and expectation of cooperation that will improve interdiction efforts. Many observers believe that PSI's "strengthened political commitment of like-minded states" to cooperate on interdiction is a successful approach to counterproliferation policy. President Obama in an April 2009 speech said that PSI, like the Global Initiative, should be turned into a "durable international institution," but how this effort is on.[68]

---

[68] Remarks by President Obama, Prague, April 5, 2009.

Appendix B. U.S. Nuclear Security Assistance to Foreign Countries

U.S. policy strategies have focused on material removal or conversion, consolidation, or improved protection at a site. Related assistance programs are spread through several federal agencies. Funding for these programs is discussed in the section "Funding for Nuclear Security Programs."

Department of Defense

The first nuclear material security assistance programs were authorized through DOD's Cooperative Threat Reduction (CTR) program in 1991 when Congress passed the Soviet Nuclear Threat Reduction Act (the Nunn-Lugar Amendment). CTR, through the Defense Threat Reduction Agency (DTRA), helps foreign governments dismantle and destroy infrastructure associated with nuclear weapons and other weapons of mass destruction, and enhances the security and safety of fissile material storage and transportation, particularly in Russia. The CTR mission also expanded to include scientist redirection programs. CTR legislation also authorized similar activities by the DOE and the State Department. The CTR program has been undergoing a transformation, and has shifted focus from Russia and the former Soviet states to a more global mission, as authorized in the FY2008 Defense Authorization bill. It also reflects a shift in threat perception as the WMD terrorism threat has gained prominence. Through these programs, DOD will play a role in strengthening nuclear security with international partners. In the Obama Administration's FY2011 budget request, the DOD has proposed $74 million for a new initiative under the CTR program to help fulfill the four-year goal. The Global Nuclear Lockdown (GNL) would include establishing regional centers of excellence for nuclear security around the world. They are meant to "assess equipment and manpower, provide material security training, and demonstrate enhanced security procedures and processes."[69] DOD also continues to work on warhead and weapons-grade material security including transportation security with foreign partners.

Department of Energy, NNSA

The DOE's National Nuclear Security Administration (NNSA) is charged with nuclear nonproliferation work overseas, including nuclear materials security upgrades, removal of sensitive material or conversion of research reactors from highly enriched uranium (HEU) to low enriched uranium (LEU) fuel. The main vehicles for this assistance are the Global Threat Reduction Initiative (GTRI) and the International Materials, Protection, Control & Accounting (MPC&A) programs. The Fissile Material Disposition program works to reduce HEU and plutonium excess to military needs in the United States and Russia. Various other NNSA programs also contribute to the mission of preventing nuclear terrorism. This report highlights only a few programs related to the security or removal of weapons-usable nuclear material.

---

[69] FY2011 Budget Estimate, Cooperative Threat Reduction Program, http://comptroller.defense.gov/defbudget/fy2011/budget_justification/pdfs/01_Operation_and_Maintenance/O_M_VOL_1_PARTS/CTR_FY11.pdf.

Security Upgrades on HEU Facilities Overseas

The United States is working on a bilateral basis with a number of countries to improve their nuclear material security practices at research reactors. NNSA's Global Research Reactor Security (GRRS) program conducts this work. It has provided security upgrades at 18 out of 22 HEU-fueled civilian research reactors in the GRRS program worldwide. There are an estimated 165 research reactors globally that continue to use HEU fuel. NNSA is working with the IAEA to ensure sustainability of the security upgrades. A September 2009 GAO report examined security upgrades under this program and found that most foreign research reactors that have received upgrades meet international standards. However, GAO visited 5 of the 22 sites and found security weaknesses. In addition, because GRRS is a voluntary program, not all foreign governments move quickly to implement or sustain the security upgrades. The summit highlighted the importance of sustainability of security upgrades at nuclear sites.

Research Reactor Conversion

The Global Threat Reduction Initiative program within the National Nuclear Security Administration is charged with HEU return and conversion at home and abroad and aims to convert 129 HEU-fueled research reactors by 2018. According to an NNSA press release, NNSA has now converted or verified the shutdown of 67 HEU-fueled research reactors of the 129 targeted by the GTRI program. This would mean that 62 are left to convert. The remaining research reactors are either used for defense programs or cannot be converted with current technology.

Nuclear Material Disposition

The NNSA's Office of Fissile Material Disposition (NA-26) manages HEU disposition programs. According to the NNSA, it has monitored the down blending into nuclear fuel of more than 375 metric tons of Russian HEU, out of the agreed 500 MT by 2013. This provides 10% of U.S. electricity.[70] NNSA has also converted 11.4 MT of Russian excess non-weapons program HEU into LEU.

Two hundred seventeen MT of excess U.S. HEU is to be downblended by various means. So far, NNSA has downblended or delivered for downblending into nuclear reactor fuel more than 124 MT of surplus U.S. HEU. An additional 17.4 MT of HEU is being downblended for the Reliable Fuel Supply Initiative. Much of an approximately 56 MT of the 217 MT total excess HEU is not yet available for disposition due to weapons dismantlement schedules. Another portion, approximately 18 MT, are discard materials and will likely be stored at waste facilities.[71]

Second Line of Defense (SLD) program

The SLD program, through international agreements, helps foreign countries establish detection capabilities for nuclear materials. Detection equipment is placed at ports of entry, border crossings, and other designated locations to detect illicit transport of nuclear materials at

---

[70] http://nnsa.energy.gov/news/2592 htm.

[71] Steve Sanders and Dean Tousley, "The U.S. Highly Enriched Uranium Disposition Program," paper presented to the Institute of Nuclear Materials Management Annual Meeting, July 2009, Tucson, AZ.

international borders. DOE has expanded the SLD effort through the Megaports Initiative, which deploys radiation detection equipment to increase detection of nuclear materials at ports of departure rather than at ports of entry.

Department of State

The State Department has a primarily facilitating and coordinating role in nuclear security and nuclear terrorism prevention efforts. The International Security and Nonproliferation (ISN) bureau manages the assistance programs that aim to help foreign governments and international organizations prevent weapons of mass destruction proliferation or terrorism. ISN does this through a variety of initiatives aimed at "denying access to WMD and related materials, expertise, and technologies" by boosting material and facility security, improving export and border controls, and strengthening inter-governmental coordination. This assistance is funded primarily through the Non-proliferation, Anti-terrorism, Demining Programs account (NADR).[72] ISN's Export Control and Related Border Security (EXBS), Nonproliferation Disarmament Fund (NDF), and Global Threat Reduction programs are the most prominent nuclear security-related assistance programs. The NADR account also includes voluntary contributions to the International Atomic Energy Agency (IAEA).

The State Department's International Security and Nonproliferation (ISN) Bureau coordinates diplomatic meetings and policy development for the Global Initiative to Combat Nuclear Terrorism, the Proliferation Security Initiative (PSI), and the G-8 Global Partnership. The Export Control and Related Border Security Assistance (EXBS) program helps the former Soviet states and other nations improve their ability to interdict nuclear smuggling and their ability to stop the illicit trafficking of all materials for weapons of mass destruction, along with dual-use goods and technologies. The EXBS program currently has projects under way in more than 30 nations.

Since gaining agreement to secure sensitive material or improve export controls are often politically sensitive and directly related to the overall bilateral relationship with a country, the State Department also plays a key role in setting up agreements with foreign countries that may be implemented by other agencies. The State Department also has notwithstanding authority through its Nonproliferation and Disarmament Fund to work in countries where nuclear material or technologies need to be removed from a site on an emergency basis.

Department of Homeland Security

Two overarching DHS initiatives, the Container Security Initiative and the Secure Freight Initiative, work to increase the likelihood that nuclear material or a nuclear weapon would be identified and interdicted during shipping. The Domestic Nuclear Detection Office also has responsibilities to coordinate federal agencies activities on setting up a global nuclear detection system.[73]

---

[72] Assessed contributions to the International Atomic Energy Agency and the Organization for the Prohibition of Chemical Weapons are from the International Organizations account.

[73] For greater detail, see CRS Report R40154, *Detection of Nuclear Weapons and Materials: Science, Technologies, Observations*, by Jonathan Medalia and CRS Report RL34574, *The Global Nuclear Detection Architecture: Issues for Congress*, by Dana A. Shea.

Appendix C. Department of Energy, Defense Nuclear Nonproliferation Appropriations

Below is a table showing appropriations for the Department of Energy's (DOE)'s National Nuclear Security Administration (NNSA) Defense Nuclear Nonproliferation (DNN) accounts from FY2007 to present. This data was compiled from DOE annual budget requests to Congress, H.Rept. 112-118, and S.Rept. 112-75. For FY2013, the DNN account includes the following programs: Nonproliferation and Verification Research and Development; Nonproliferation and International Security; International Nuclear Material Protection and Cooperation; Fissile Materials Disposition; and the Global Threat Reduction Initiative. The reader should note that subprograms are listed below the shaded program totals.

Table C-1. Defense Nuclear Nonproliferation Appropriations FY2007-2013

(in $ thousands)

	FY2007	FY2008	FY2009	FY2010	FY2011	FY2012 Request	FY2012 House Passed [H.R. 2354]	FY2012 Senate Reported [S.Rept. 112-75]	FY2012 Enacted	FY2013 Request
Nonproliferation and Verification Research & Devt	265,197	387,196	356,281	311,274	355,407	417,598	346,150	417,598	354,150	548,186
Proliferation Detection	148,863	224,445	195,400	175,813	229,427	233,975	233,975	233,975	222,150	240,536
Homeland Security Proliferation Detection	[48,708]	[50,000]	[50,000]	[50,000]	[50,000]	[50,000]	[50,000]	[50,000]	[50,000]	[50,000]
Nuclear Detonation Detection	105,389	132,484	142,421	135,461	125,980	127,800	127,800	127,800	132,000	157,650
Domestic Uranium Enrichment RD&D	0	0	0	0	0	0	0	0	0	150,000
University of California Pension Payments	0	0	0	0	0	55,823	0[b]	55,823	0	0
Supporting Activities	3,025	5,495	0	0	0	0	0	0	0	0
Construction	7,920	24,772	18,460	0	0	0	0	0	0	0
Nonproliferation and International Security	128,911	149,993	150,000	187,202	147,494	161,833	161,833	155,305	153,594	150,119
Dismantlement and Transparency	38,967	45,709	47,529	72,763	49,207	0	0	0	0	0
Global Security Engagement	50,232	50,912	44,076	50,708	47,289	0	0	0	0	0
International Regimes and Agreements	31,787	44,444	40,793	42,703	39,824	0	0	0	0	0
Treaties and Agreements	2,495	3,879	17,602	21,028	11,174	0	0	0	0	0
International Emergency Management Cooperation	5,430	5,049	0	0	0	0	0	0	0	0

	FY2007	FY2008	FY2009	FY2010	FY2011	FY2012 Request	FY2012 House Passed [H.R. 2354]	FY2012 Senate Reported [S.Rept. 112-75]	FY2012 Enacted	FY2013 Request
Nuclear Safeguards and Security	0	0	0	0	0	53,925	53,925	-	54,897	54,723
Nuclear Controls	0	0	0	0	0	48,496	48,496	44,996c	47,444	45,420
Nuclear Verification	0	0	0	0	0	46,995	46,995	-	39,969	40,566
Nonproliferation Policy	0	0	0	0	0	12,417	12,417	-	11,284	9,410
International Nuclear Materials Protection and Cooperation	597,646	624,482	460,592	572,749	578,633	571,639	496,465	571,639	569,927	311,000
Navy Complex	17,300	13,268	30,316	33,880	34,332	33,664	33,664	33,664	33,664	39,860
Strategic Rocket Forces/12th Main Directorate	152,843	121,912	51,767	48,646	51,359	59,105	59,105	59,105	59,105	8,300
Weapons Material Protection (formerly Rosatom Weapons Complex)	94,005	79,114	76,070	71,517	93,318	80,735	80,735	80,735	80,735	46,975
Civilian Nuclear Sites	52,700	54,188	45,542	63,481	53,027	59,117	59,117	59,117	59,117	60,092
Material Consolidation and Conversion	23,828	19,488	21,560	13,611	13,867	14,306	14,306	14,306	14,306	17,000
National Infrastructure and Sustainability (formerly National Programs and Sustainability)	65,081	69,632	54,901	68,469	60,928	60,928	60,928	60,928	60,928	46,199
Second Line of Defense	191,889	266,880	174,844	272,446	265,163	263,784	188,610	263,784	262,072	92,574
Funds from International Contributions	0	0	5,592	699	6,639	0	n/a	n/a		
Fissile Materials Disposition	470,062	66,235	41,774	701,900	802,198	890,153	694,053	751,489	685,386	921,305
U.S. Surplus Materials Disposition	470,062	66,235	40,774	700,900	802,173	879,979	683,879	750,489	684,386	917,517

	FY2007	FY2008	FY2009	FY2010	FY2011	FY2012 Request	FY2012 House Passed [H.R. 2354]	FY2012 Senate Reported [S.Rept. 112-75]	FY2012 Enacted	FY2013 Request
U.S. Pu Disposition^d	57,415	0	0	91,659	200,400	274,790	244,690	224,000	205,632	498,979
U.S. Uranium Disposition	86,898	66,235	39,274	34,691	25,985	26,435	16,435	26,435	26,000	29,736
Supporting Activities	14,960	0	1,500	312	0	0	0	0	0	0
Construction^d	310,789	0	0	574,238	575,788	578,754	422,754	500,054	452,754	388,802
MOX Fuel Fab	262,500	0	0	504,238		385,172	385,172	435,172	435,172	388,802
Pit Dis.	32,789	0	0	0		176,000	20,000	47,300	0	0
Waste Solid.	15,500	0	0	70,000		17,582	17,582	17,582	17,582	0
Russian Materials Disposition	0	0	1,000	1,000	25	10,174	10,174	1,000	1,000	3,788
Global Threat Reduction	131,234	193,225	404,640	333,500	444,689	508,269	388,269	508,269	498,000	466,021
HEU Reactor Conversion	32,096	33,819	76,706	102,772	100,968	148,269	78,269	148,269	148,269	161,000
Nuclear and Radiological Material Removal	51,489	67,759	182,761	144,834	221,296	257,000	237,000	257,000	246,731	200,000
RRRFR	30,025	38,896	0	0	0	0	0	0	0	0
FRRSNF	6,340	9,887	0	0	0	0	0	0	0	0
Emerging Threats Gap Material	5,683	5,466	0	0	0	0	0	0	0	0
USRTR	9,441	13,510	0	0	0	0	0	0	0	0
Rus-Origin Nuclear Material Removal	0	0	123,083	94,167	159,031	147,000	147,000	147,000	147,000	102,000
U.S.-Origin Nuclear Material Removal	0	0	8,331	9,889	4,420	9,000	9,000	9,000	9,000	5,000

	FY2007	FY2008	FY2009	FY2010	FY2011	FY2012 Request	FY2012 House Passed [H.R. 2354]	FY2012 Senate Reported [S.Rept. 112-75]	FY2012 Enacted	FY2013 Request
Gap Nuclear Material Removal	0	0	4,982	9,111	9,289	56,000	56,000	56,000	45,731	61,000
Emerging Threats Nuclear Material Removal	0	0	7,600	5,556	8,768	5,000	5,000	5,000	5,000	5,000
International Radiological Material Removal	0	0	21,702	8,333	20,660	20,000	20,000	20,000	20,000	8,000
Domestic Radiological Material Removal	0	0	17,063	17,778	19,128	20,000	0	20,000	20,000	19,000
Nuclear and Radiological Material Protection	45,910	91,647	135,533	85,894	113,717	103,000	73,000	103,000	103,000	105,021
Kazakhstan Spent Fuel	17,934	43,098	0	0	0	0	0	0	0	0
Global Research Reactor Security	1,000	3,557	0	0	0	0	0	0	0	0
IRTR	26,976	44,992	0	0	0	0	0	0	0	0
BN-350 Nuclear Material Protection	0	0	50,977	9,109	1,840	2,000	2,000	2,000	2,000	0
International Material Protection	0	0	42,909	41,463	46,573	50,000	50,000	50,000	50,000	50,000
Domestic Material Protection	0	0	41,647	35,322	65,304	51,000	21,000	51,000	51,000	55,021
Funds from International Contributions	1,739	0	9,640	0	8,708	0	0	0		

	FY2007	FY2008	FY2009	FY2010	FY2011	FY2012 Request	FY2012 House Passed [H.R. 2354]	FY2012 Senate Reported [S.Rept. 112-75]	FY2012 Enacted	FY2013 Request
Elimination of Weapons-Grade Pu Production	231,152	179,940	141,299	24,507	0	0	0	0	0	0
International Fuel Bank	0	49,545	0	0	0	0	0	0	0	0
Legacy Contractor Pensions	0	0	0	0	0	0	55,823	55,823	55,823	62,000
Congressionally Directed Projects	[2,100]	7,380	1,903	250	0	0	0	0	0	
Defense Nuclear Nonproliferation Total	1,824,202	1,334,922	1,545,071	2,131,382	2,281,371	2,549,492	2,091,770e	2,383,300g	2,295,880	2,458,631

Source: CRS-compiled information from DOE annual budget requests to Congress, H.Rept. 112-118, and S.Rept. 112-75.

a. FY2011 subprogram amounts were not available at the time this was prepared, except for subprograms under Fissile Material Disposition.

b. H.Rept. 112-118 says that the committee recommends no payments for this program: "$71,448 below the request." The report recommends the pension fund instead be funded solely in a separately identified budgetary line within Weapons Activities. This became Legacy Contractor Pensions under Defense Nuclear Nonproliferation for FY2013.

c. Reflects a reduction of $3,500,000 for the Global Initiatives for Proliferation Prevention. Additional reduction of $3,028,000 was not specified in the Senate report.

d. FY2008 and FY2009 appropriations moved funding for the Mixed Oxide Fuel Fabrication Facility (MFFF) from the DNN Fissile Materials Disposition program to DOE's Nuclear Energy program and funding for the Pit Disassembly and Conversion Facility (PDCF)/Waste Solidification Building (WSB) to NNSA's Weapons Activities, Directed Stockpile Work program. The MFFF and WSB were moved back to the DNN Fissile Materials Disposition program in FY2010. The PDCF was moved to DNN Fissile Material Disposition in FY2011.

e. This total includes a proposed $30 million rescission of prior year unobligated balances and $35 million increase for the GTRI HEU Research Reactor Conversion account by amendment (H.Amdt. 648).

f. This total includes a $45 million rescission of prior year unobligated balances.

g. This total includes a proposed $21 million rescission of prior year unobligated balances.

Author Contact Information

Mary Beth Nikitin
Specialist in Nonproliferation
mnikitin@crs.loc.gov, 7-7745